OFFICIAL PAST PAPERS WITH ANSWERS

HIGHER

ART & DESIGN
2009-2012

First exam published in 2009.
Published by Bright Red Publishing Ltd, 6 Stafford Street, Edinburgh EH3 7AU
tel: 0131 220 5804 fax: 0131 220 6710 info@brightredpublishing.co.uk www.brightredpublishing.co.uk

ISBN 978-1-84948-281-3

A CIP Catalogue record for this book is available from the British Library.

Bright Red Publishing is grateful to the copyright holders, as credited on the final page of the Question Section, for permission to use their material. Every effort has been made to trace the copyright holders and to obtain their permission for the use of copyright material. Bright Red Publishing will be happy to receive information allowing us to rectify any error or omission in future editions.

[BLANK PAGE]

X223/301

NATIONAL
QUALIFICATIONS
2009

FRIDAY, 5 JUNE
1.00 PM – 2.30 PM

ART AND DESIGN
HIGHER

There are **two** sections to this paper, Section 1—Art Studies; and Section 2—Design Studies.

Each section is worth 30 marks.

Candidates should attempt questions as follows:

In SECTION 1 answer **ONE full question** (parts (*a*) **and** (*b*))

and

In SECTION 2 answer **ONE full question** (parts (*a*) **and** (*b*)).

You may use sketches to illustrate your answers.

SECTION 1—ART STUDIES

Instructions

Read your selected question and notes on the illustration carefully.

Answer **ONE full question from this section**: parts **(a)** and **(b)**.

Self Portrait by Stephen Conroy (2005)
oil on canvas (207 × 147 cm)

Marks

1. Portraiture

(a) Discuss the visual impact of this self portrait in terms of **at least two** of the
following:

   pose;   *symbolism*;   *composition*;   *use of visual elements.*

   What is your opinion of this painting?   **10**

(b) Referring to examples of portraiture by **two** artists from different movements
or periods, explain how the artists have portrayed the character of their sitters.
Explain why the artists are considered to be important in the development of
portraiture.   **20**

SECTION 1—ART STUDIES (continued)

Tourists II by Duane Hanson (1988) the figures are lifesize.
This sculpture is made of autobody filler, fibreglass and mixed media
with real clothes and accessories.

Marks

2. Figure Composition

(a) Discuss the sculptor's approach to figure composition. Comment on **at least two** of the following:

scale; *materials*; *composition*; *detail*.

Explain how successfully you think the figures interact with each other and with the viewer.

10

(b) Discuss examples of figure composition by **two** artists from different movements or periods. Comment on the working methods used by the artists to communicate their ideas. How important are the artists in the development of figure composition?

20

SECTION 1—ART STUDIES (continued)

Still Life by Richard Diebenkorn (1967)
black ink, Conté crayon, charcoal and ballpoint pen on paper (35·2 × 42·5 cm)

Marks

3. Still Life

(a) Analyse this still life by explaining which features of the work you admire and think are successful. Contrast them with aspects you think are less successful.

10

(b) Discuss examples of still life by **two** artists from different movements or periods. To what extent do you consider the examples to be typical of each artist's style or associated movement? Explain why they are considered important artists.

20

SECTION 1—ART STUDIES (continued)

Glencoe by Horatio McCulloch (1864)
oil on canvas (110 × 183 cm)

Marks

4.   Natural Environment

(a)   Outline the methods used by the artist to create a feeling of grandeur in this
painting. Refer to the visual elements in your response. What is your opinion
of the painting?

10

(b)   Discuss examples of work by **two** artists from different movements or
periods. Explain how the artists have responded to the natural environment
by referring to choice of subject, media handling and style. How important
are the artists in the development of this type of work?

20

[Turn over

SECTION 1—ART STUDIES (continued)

London Bridge by Andre Derain (1906)
oil on canvas (66 × 99 cm)

Marks

5.   Built Environment

(a)   Discuss the composition of this painting. Comment on the artist's media handling and use of visual elements. What is your opinion of this painting?   **10**

(b)   Select **two** artists from different movements or periods. Refer to examples of work by the artists and discuss their treatment of the built environment. Comment on the artists' choice of subject matter, style and working methods. Explain which aspects of their work have made them important artists.   **20**

SECTION 1—ART STUDIES (continued)

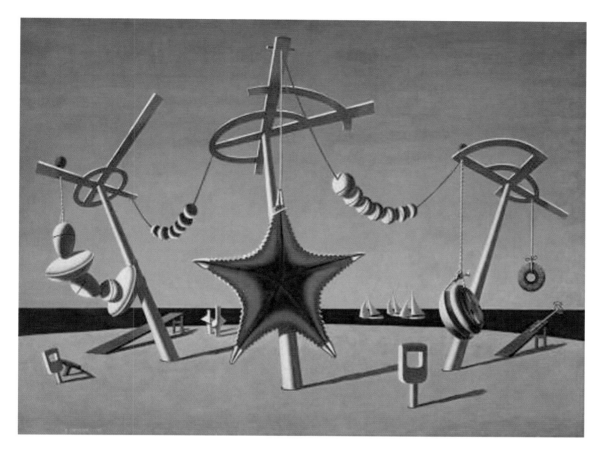

The Beached Margin by Edward Wadsworth (1937)
tempera paint on linen (71 × 101 cm)

Marks

6. Fantasy and Imagination

(*a*) Describe the methods used by the artist to create this unusual scene. Explain which aspects of this painting you find interesting and you think contributes to its success as a work of fantasy and imagination.   **10**

(*b*) Select **two** artists from different movements or periods. Briefly describe examples of their work within this theme. Discuss the methods used by the artists to create works of fantasy and imagination. Why are they considered important artists?   **20**

[Turn over

SECTION 2—DESIGN STUDIES

Instructions

Read your selected question and notes on the illustration carefully.

Answer **ONE full question from this section**: parts (*a*) and (*b*).

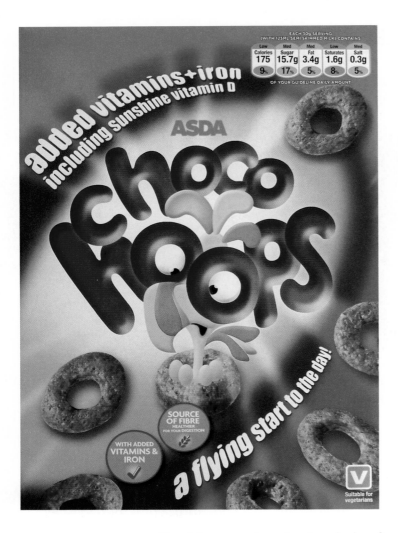 

Breakfast cereal packaging design for ASDA (2007)

Marks

7. Graphic Design

(*a*) Visual impact and communication are important issues in graphic design. Comment on each of these issues in relation to this package design. In your opinion how successful is the design and why?

10

(*b*) Select **two** graphic designers whose work is from different periods or in different styles. With reference to examples, identify the main design issues in their work. Explain why they are considered to be important graphic designers.

20

SECTION 2—DESIGN STUDIES (continued)

Gramophone designed for Pathé (1908), height 67 cm.

This early music system is operated by a clockwork mechanism which requires the user to wind up the handle.

Marks

8. Product Design

(a) What do you think the designer considered were important issues when designing this product? How does this gramophone compare with today's music systems?

10

(b) A successful product

"*has simplicity and quality, does what is demanded of it, is economical to use, easy to maintain . . . . It also sells best and looks good*".

Select **two** designers working in different periods or styles and discuss this statement, or any part of it, in relation to their work. Why are they important designers?

20

[Turn over

SECTION 2—DESIGN STUDIES (continued)

Barajas Airport Terminal, Madrid, designed by Richard Rodgers Partnership (2006).
Materials: aluminium, glass, wood, polished stone and tempered glass floor tiles.

Marks

9. Interior Design

(a) With particular reference to space, structure and the use of light, how visually appealing is this interior design? Do you think it successfully fulfils its function as a contemporary airport terminal?   **10**

(b) Select **two** designers working in different periods or whose approaches to design are contrasting. By referring to examples of their work, explain how they have met the challenges of creating innovative interior spaces. Why are they regarded as exciting and/or influential designers?   **20**

SECTION 2—DESIGN STUDIES (continued)

The Opera House, Paris, designed by Charles Garnier (1861–1875)

Marks

10. Environmental/Architectural Design

(*a*) What are the most striking aesthetic features of this architectural design? Identify what you think the architect's main design considerations would have been in relation to the function of this opera house.   **10**

(*b*) Discuss the work of **two** architectural/environmental designers working in different periods or in contrasting styles. With reference to materials, form and function explain why they are important in this area of design.   **20**

[Turn over

SECTION 2—DESIGN STUDIES (continued)

Wrist watch designed by Boucheron (1942).
Materials: gold set with diamonds and sapphires.

11. Jewellery Design

Marks

(a) Comment on this jewellery design referring to the designer's choice of materials and handling of form. How well do you think this wrist watch fulfils its function?

10

(b) Select **two** jewellery designers from different periods or who work in contrasting styles. Discuss how they have used their sources of inspiration and materials to create exciting and original jewellery designs. Why are they regarded as important designers?

20

SECTION 2—DESIGN STUDIES (continued)

Photo by Bishin Jumonji © 1971
as seen in *The Art of Zandra Rhodes.*

Dinosaur coat and hat designed by Zandra Rhodes (1971).
Materials: wool felt, printed silk lining and appliqué silk flowers.

Marks

12. Textile/Fashion Design

(*a*) Analyse the important design features of this coat and hat with reference to fabric, function and style. What is your opinion of this outfit?   **10**

(*b*) Choose **two** textile or fashion designers whose work is from different periods or in different styles. Discuss why they are regarded as innovative, referring to examples of their work. Why do you think they are influential in this area of design?   **20**

[END OF QUESTION PAPER]

[BLANK PAGE]

SECTION 1—ART STUDIES (continued)

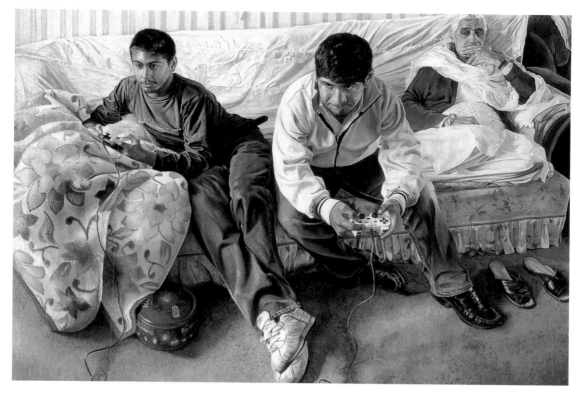

Gran Turismo[1] by Megan Davies (2005)
oil on canvas (125 × 172 cm)

[1]*Gran Turismo* is a computer game.

2. Figure Composition

Marks

(a) Discuss the composition of this painting. Comment on how the artist has used **two or more** of the following:

setting;   *mood*;   *media handling*;   *colour*;   *tone*.

How has the artist conveyed the interrelationship of the figures?   **10**

(b) Discuss examples of figure compositions by **two** artists from different periods or movements. Refer to their style, use of composition and media handling. Explain how these artists have contributed to the development of figure composition.   **20**

[Turn over

SECTION 1—ART STUDIES (continued)

Maple and Chocolate by Ralph Goings (2004)
oil on canvas (23 × 30·5 cm)

Marks

3.   Still Life

(*a*)   Analyse this painting in terms of composition. Refer to the artist's handling of media, colour and tone. What is your opinion of this painting?   **10**

(*b*)   Discuss still lifes by **two** artists from different periods or movements. Focus on their style, use of composition and media handling. Comment on these artists' contributions to the development of still life.   **20**

SECTION 1—ART STUDIES (continued)

Frosty Morning, Trow Hill by Anne Redpath (1935)
oil on plywood (78 × 90 cm)

Marks

4. Natural Environment

(*a*) Discuss the atmosphere created by the artist in this painting. In your answer, refer to composition, use of colour and media handling. What is your opinion of this painting?   **10**

(*b*) Compare and contrast the work of **two** artists, from different periods or movements, who have responded to the natural environment. Comment on their working methods. Explain why you consider them to be important artists.   **20**

[Turn over

SECTION 1—ART STUDIES (continued)

Street Study outside a School by The Boyle Family (1988)
cast and painted fibreglass (182·5 × 182·5 × 15–30 cm)

This 3-D artwork was made by taking a cast of a section of ground.

Marks

5. Built Environment

(*a*) Discuss the artists' choice of subject matter and their treatment of it. In your answer, comment on the use of materials, scale, colour and texture.

What is your opinion of this method of creating an artwork? **10**

(*b*) Discuss works, inspired by the built environment, by **two** artists from different periods or movements. Comment on their working methods and the resulting atmosphere created. Explain why you consider them to be influential artists. **20**

SECTION 1—ART STUDIES (continued)

Life from *Death Life Hope Fear* by Gilbert and George (1984)
mixed media (422 × 250 cm)

Marks

6. Fantasy and Imagination

(*a*) Discuss the content and composition of this artwork. Comment on the artists' use of colour and structure. What is your interpretation of this work?   **10**

(*b*) Compare the work of **two** artists, from different periods or movements, who have worked within the area of fantasy and imagination. With reference to these artists' work, comment on their use of imagery to communicate ideas. Discuss their contribution to the development of this area of art.   **20**

[Turn over

SECTION 2—DESIGN STUDIES

Instructions

Read your selected question and notes on the illustration carefully.

Answer **ONE full question from this section**: parts **(a)** and **(b)**.

Vertigo–film poster designed by Saul Bass (1958)

The word Vertigo means: dizziness, light headedness

Marks

7.   Graphic Design

(a)   Discuss the effectiveness of this poster by referring to colour, imagery and lettering. What does the designer communicate about the film?   **10**

(b)   Refer to the work of **two** graphic designers working in different periods or styles. What, in your view, are the main priorities in their work? Why are they considered influential in the area of graphic design?   **20**

SECTION 2—DESIGN STUDIES (continued)

Lego–plastic construction toy, designed by Ole Kirk and Godtfred Christiansen (1958)

Marks

8. Product Design

(*a*) What important design issues, do you think, were considered in the development of this product? Why do you think it is still a successful toy today? **10**

(*b*) Compare the work of **two** product designers working in different periods or styles. Discuss how effective they have been in responding to the changing needs of society. Why are they regarded as important designers? **20**

[Turn over

SECTION 2—DESIGN STUDIES (continued)

Cookery classroom, Scotland Street School, designed by Charles Rennie Mackintosh (1906)

Marks

9. Interior Design

(a) In your opinion, what issues have been considered in the designing of this cookery classroom? How does this interior differ from a typical modern food technology classroom?

10

(b) Select **two** interior designers working in different styles or periods. With reference to examples of their work, show how influences, materials and changing fashions have enabled each designer to develop an individual style. Why are their designs of interior spaces considered important?

20

SECTION 2—DESIGN STUDIES (continued)

Trellick Tower, London, designed by Erno Goldfinger (1972)
Materials: reinforced concrete and glass.

Marks

10. Environmental/Architectural Design

(a) "Most modern buildings hate people." Discuss this statement in relation to this building. Refer to the use of materials, the building's appearance and its function as a block of dwelling flats.

10

(b) Select **two** architects or environmental designers from different periods or who work in contrasting styles. Discuss the characteristics of their work by referring to **at least two** of the following:

function; influences; working methods; aesthetics; innovation.

Why are they important designers?

20

SECTION 2—DESIGN STUDIES (continued)

Regenerat–assembled pendant by Wahei Ikezawa (1994).
Materials: stone; iron; brass (60 × 30 cm).

Marks

11. Jewellery Design

(*a*)   Comment on the designer's inspiration and use of materials in this striking piece of jewellery. How practical do you think it would be to wear this neckpiece? Give reasons for your views.

10

(*b*)   Select **two** jewellery designers working in different periods or whose approaches to design are different. With reference to examples of their work, discuss their influences, working methods and styles. Why are they recognised for their contributions to jewellery design?

20

X223/301

NATIONAL   THURSDAY, 2 JUNE   ART AND DESIGN
QUALIFICATIONS   1.00 PM – 2.30 PM   HIGHER
2011

There are **two** sections to this paper, Section 1—Art Studies; and Section 2—Design Studies.

Each section is worth 30 marks.

Candidates should attempt questions as follows:

In SECTION 1 answer **ONE full question** (parts (*a*) **and** (*b*))

and

In SECTION 2 answer **ONE full question** (parts (*a*) **and** (*b*)).

You may use sketches to illustrate your answers.

SECTION 1—ART STUDIES

Instructions

Read your selected question and notes on the illustration carefully.

Answer **ONE full question** from this section: parts **(a)** and **(b)**.

My Mother, Bolton Abbey, Yorkshire, Nov 1982
photographic collage (120·7 × 69·9 cm)

Marks

1.   Portraiture

(a)   "Anything simple always interests me." David Hockney

Discuss this quotation in relation to **at least two** of the following:

composition;   *media handling*;   *colour*;   *atmosphere*.

What is your opinion of this approach to portraiture?   **10**

(b)   Evaluate successful examples of portraiture by **two** artists from different periods
or movements. Comment on each artist's working methods and explain how
these have helped to capture the character of the sitter in their work. Why do
you consider these artists to be significant in the development of portraiture?   **20**

SECTION 1—ART STUDIES (continued)

The Tennis Party by John Lavery (1885)
oil on canvas (77 × 183 cm)

2. Figure Composition

Marks

(a) Discuss the composition of this painting. Comment on the methods used by the artist to convey a sense of movement and atmosphere in this figure composition. What is your opinion of this artwork?

10

(b) Compare examples of figure composition by **two** artists from different periods or movements. With reference to each artist's choice of subject matter and use of the visual elements, explain which aspects of their work you consider to be successful. What have these artists contributed to the development of figure composition?

20

[Turn over

SECTION 1—ART STUDIES (continued)

Table by a Window by Jean Metzinger (1917)
oil on canvas (81·3 × 65·1 cm)

Marks

3. **Still Life**

(a) Discuss the methods used by the artist to create this artwork. In your answer, discuss **two or more** of the following:

composition; *colour*; *form*; *tone*.

In your opinion, how does this artwork compare with more conventional approaches to still life? **10**

(b) Discuss examples of still life by **two** artists from different periods or movements. Comment on their choice of subject matter, composition and handling of materials. How have these artists made an important contribution to the development of still life? **20**

SECTION 1—ART STUDIES (continued)

Due to copyright restrictions, the image has been removed. It can be viewed at: http://www.toledomuseum.org/ by clicking the link to 'Our Collection'. Next, in the 'Quick Search' box on the left-hand side please type in 'Andrew Wyeth', then click on the 'objects' link to view the image.

The Hunter by Andrew Wyeth (1943)
tempera paint on panel (83·8 × 86·4 cm)

Marks

4. **Natural Environment**

(a) Discuss Wyeth's response to the natural environment in this artwork. In your answer, refer to **at least two** of the following:

composition;   *perspective*;   *colour*;   *atmosphere*;   *media handling*.

Explain your personal reaction to this work.   **10**

(b) "I work with nature, although in completely new terms."

With reference to this quotation, discuss the work of **two** artists from different periods or movements who have responded, in an innovative way, to the natural environment. Explain why you consider them to be significant artists.   **20**

[Turn over

SECTION 1—ART STUDIES (continued)

Cabina[1] *NY* by Jose Luis Corella (2006)
oil on board (117 × 98 cm)

[1]*Cabina* means telephone box.

Marks

5. Built Environment

(a) Comment on the composition and subject matter of this painting.

With reference to the artist's use of the visual elements, discuss his success in creating a sense of atmosphere in this urban image.   **10**

(b) Compare the work of **two** artists from different periods or movements who have been inspired by the built environment. With reference to examples of their work, comment on their different approaches and styles. Explain each artist's contribution to the development of this area of art.   **20**

SECTION 1—ART STUDIES (continued)

Saint Bride by John Duncan (1913)
tempera paint on canvas (122·3 × 144·5 cm)

6. Fantasy and Imagination

Marks

(a) Discuss the methods used by the artist to create this work of fantasy and imagination. In your answer refer to **at least two** of the following:

composition; pattern; colour; atmosphere; media handling.

What is your personal interpretation of this work? **10**

(b) Select and discuss examples of work by **two** artists from different periods or movements who have worked within the area of fantasy and imagination.

With reference to the artists' choice of themes and working methods, comment on the impact of their work in the development of this area of art. **20**

[Turn over

SECTION 2—DESIGN STUDIES

Instructions

Read your selected question and notes on the illustration carefully.

Answer **ONE full question** from this section: parts (*a*) and (*b*).

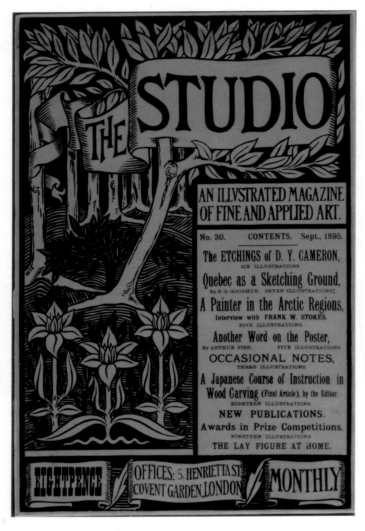

Magazine cover designed by Aubrey Beardsley (1895)

Marks

7. Graphic Design

(*a*) Explain how the designer has used imagery, lettering and layout to create visual impact in this magazine cover. How does this design differ from modern magazine covers?   **10**

(*b*) Select **two** graphic designers from different periods or whose styles are contrasting. Referring to examples of their work, explain how they communicate their ideas effectively with their target market. Why are they considered to be important in the development of graphic design?   **20**

SECTION 2—DESIGN STUDIES (continued)

Cross-section of car interior

Morris Mini-Minor designed by Sir Alec Issigonis (1959)

Marks

8. Product Design

(a) Function and style are important issues in the development of a design concept. Comment on each of these in relation to the Mini. Explain why you think this has been such an enduring and successful car design. **10**

(b) Select **two** product designers who have worked in different periods or styles. With reference to examples of their work, explain how they have responded to consumer requirements. Why are they regarded as important designers? **20**

SECTION 2—DESIGN STUDIES (continued)

Topshop store in New York designed by Dalziel and Pow (2009)

Marks

9. Interior Design

(a) Comment on the key issues that have been considered in the designing of this interior. Explain how the designers have used structure, materials and lighting to create a contemporary retail space. What is your opinion of this design? **10**

(b) Select **two** interior designers working in different periods or styles. With reference to their work, discuss why they are considered to be important. Explain how they have used their creativity and their sources of inspiration to develop their own individual styles. **20**

SECTION 2—DESIGN STUDIES (continued)

Interior of lounge area

View of rear of Centre and
surrounding area

Maggie's Centre, Dundee, designed by Frank Gehry (2004)
Materials: stainless steel roof, reinforced concrete and wood.

Maggie's Centres are drop-in facilities for people affected by cancer.

Marks

10. Environmental/Architectural Design

(a) Discuss ways in which Gehry combines form and function in this design. Compare the aesthetic appeal of this design to those medical centres, surgeries or hospitals known to you. What is your personal opinion of this design?

10

(b) Select **two** environmental/architectural designers working in different periods or in contrasting styles. By referring to examples of their work, show how their vision and working methods have contributed to the development of this area of design.

Why are they acknowledged as important designers?

20

SECTION 2—DESIGN STUDIES (continued)

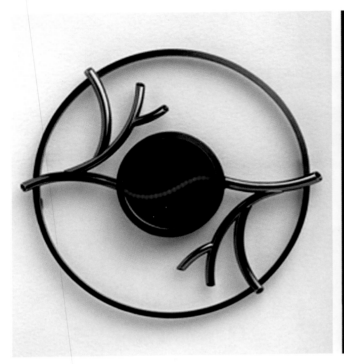 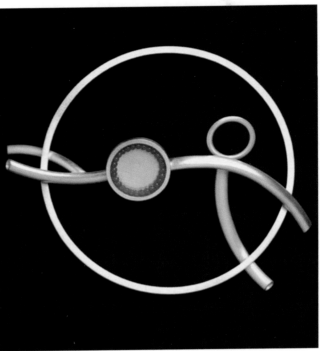

Brooches from the *Artery* series designed by Dorothy Hogg (2005)
Materials: silver and coral
diameter: 11 cm

Dorothy Hogg's work springs intuitively from her experience of life and change. Her work in the Artery Series is concerned with ideas of flow within and through matter. The pieces are meticulously constructed in sheet silver to create hollow forms that have visual weight without the expected physical density, while the colour red is used for its powerful symbolic value. (photographer: John K. McGregor)

Marks

11. Jewellery Design

(a)   Discuss Dorothy Hogg's sources of inspiration, handling of form and choice of materials for these brooches. In your opinion, what are the most striking features of these designs?

10

(b)   Choose **two** designers working in different periods or whose approaches to jewellery design are contrasting. Discuss their work in terms of originality, function and style. Why are they highly respected designers?

20

SECTION 1—ART STUDIES (continued)

Leaf Horn (1986) by Andy Goldsworthy
horsechestnut leaves and thorns

Marks

4. Natural Environment

(a) Discuss the methods and materials used by the artist to create this piece of sculpture. How do you think it challenges traditional responses to the natural environment? What is your personal opinion of this piece?

10

(b) With reference to examples, discuss the work of **two** artists, working in different movements or periods, who have produced artworks inspired by the natural environment. Refer to their individual approaches and sources of inspiration. Describe, in detail, why these artists are important and how they have influenced other artists.

20

SECTION 1—ART STUDIES (continued)

Edinburgh (from Salisbury Crags) (c. 1927) by William Crozier
oil on canvas (71 × 92 cm)

Marks

5. Built Environment

(*a*) Discuss the artist's choice of subject matter and explain the techniques used to communicate the drama of this scene. With reference to the visual elements, discuss your opinion of this artwork.   **10**

(*b*) Discuss the sources of inspiration of **two** artists, working in different movements or periods, who have created work based on the built environment. With reference to examples, describe the artists' working methods and explain why these are typical of their styles. Explain, in detail, why these artists are regarded as important and influential.   **20**

SECTION 1—ART STUDIES (continued)

Antony Gormley, *Angel of the North* (1998) Cor-ten steel[1] (20 metres high, 54 metres wide)

[1]Cor-ten steel—a type of steel which oxidises naturally to an orange-brown colour but despite its rusted appearance is actually resistant to corrosion.

This sculpture stands on a hillside above the town of Gateshead beside a busy motorway.

Marks

6. Fantasy and Imagination

(*a*) Discuss to what extent you consider this to be a successful sculpture for this specific site. In doing so, refer to the scale of the work and the artist's use of symbolism.   **10**

(*b*) Select **two** artists from different movements or periods whose work is within the theme of fantasy and imagination. Referring to examples of work, discuss the methods used by the artists to communicate their ideas. Explain to what extent the artists are influential in the development of this type of artwork.   **20**

[Turn over

SECTION 2—DESIGN STUDIES

Instructions

Read your selected question and notes on the illustration carefully.

Answer **ONE full question** from this section: parts **(a)** and **(b)**.

Poster for the 1936 Berlin Olympic Games (1936) designed by Franz Wurbel

Marks

7. Graphic Design

(a) What ideas, do you think, Wurbel is trying to communicate through this poster? Discuss the success of the design by referring to **at least two** of the following:

imagery; *layout*; *text*; *colour*; *visual impact*. **10**

(b) Choose examples of graphic design by **two** designers working in different styles or periods that show successful methods of communication. Discuss their working methods and explain why these examples are typical of their style. Explain why these designers are regarded as important and influential. **20**

SECTION 2—DESIGN STUDIES (continued)

Armchair (1823) designed by Augustus Charles Pugin
Materials include carved and gilded mahogany

Marks

8. Product Design

(*a*) Function, style and target market are important considerations in the development of product design. Comment on each of these in relation to this armchair. How does this design differ from modern chairs?

10

(*b*) Choose **two** designers working in different styles or periods who have designed successful products. With reference to examples of their work, describe how they were innovative and how they used technology to create their designs. Explain, in detail, why these designers are regarded as influential.

20

SECTION 2—DESIGN STUDIES (continued)

Kelvingrove Art Gallery and Museum designed by Sir J W Simpson and
E J Milner Allen (1902, refurbished 2006)

Mark

9. Interior Design

(a) Identify the key design issues that have been considered in the designing of this interior. In your opinion, how effective is this exhibition space? Give reasons for your answer.   **10**

(b) Choose **two** interior designers working in different styles or periods. Using examples of their work discuss the key issues of their designs. Give reasons why these designers are regarded as influential and important.   **20**

SECTION 2—DESIGN STUDIES (continued)

Millennium Bridge, Gateshead, (2001) designed by architects, Wilkinson Eyre and structural engineers, Gifford

The bridge pivots upwards to allow tall boats and ships to pass underneath

Marks

10. Environmental/Architectural Design

(a) Evaluate the success of this design. Identify and discuss the key design issues of form and function which would have been considered.

10

(b) Select examples of the work of **two** environmental/architectural designers working in different styles or periods. Discuss, in detail, their use of materials and form to create innovative designs. With reference to specific examples, explain why these two designers are regarded as influential and important.

20

SECTION 2—DESIGN STUDIES (continued)

Corsage ornament (brooch) (1902) designed by Georges Fouquet
Materials: gold, enamel, emeralds and pearls (19 × 12·5 cm)

Marks

11. Jewellery Design

(a) Discuss this design by referring to **at least two** of the following:

influences; *craftsmanship*; *use of materials*; *style*.

Would this brooch be suitable for today's fashion market? Give reasons for your opinions. **10**

(b) Select examples of jewellery design by **two** designers working in different styles or periods. Discuss their working methods, use of materials and understanding of their markets. With reference to examples of their work, explain why these designers are influential and important. **20**

SECTION 2—DESIGN STUDIES (continued)

Uniform for fast food chain outlet (2008) designed by Bruce Oldfield

Marks

12. Textile/Fashion Design

(*a*) Identify the design issues Bruce Oldfield had to consider in updating this uniform. Do you think the design (left) is an improvement on the earlier design (right)? Give reasons for your views.

10

(*b*) Choose examples of textile or fashion designs by **two** designers working in different styles or periods. Discuss fully the design issues involved in the success of your chosen designs. Comment on the innovative aspects of the designers' working methods. Why are these designers regarded as influential and important?

20

[*END OF QUESTION PAPER*]

Acknowledgements

Permission has been sought from all relevant copyright holders and Bright Red Publishing is grateful for the use of the following:

The painting 'Self Portrait' by Stephen Conroy © Stephen Conroy UK/Culture and Sport Glasgow (Museums) (2009 page 2);

The sculpture 'Tourists II' by Duane Hanson © Estate of Duane Hanson/Licensed by VAGA, New York, DACS, London 2012, (2009 page 3);

The painting 'Still Life, Cigarette Butts and Glasses' by Richard Diebenkorn (1967). Image courtesy of the Board of Trustees, National Gallery of Art, Washington © The Richard Diebenkorn Foundation (2009 page 4);

The painting 'Glencoe' by Horatio McCulloch © Glasgow Museums. Licensor www.scran.ac.uk (2009 page 5);

The painting 'London Bridge' by André Derain © ADAGP, Paris and DACS, London 2012. Digital image © (2012) The Museum of Modern Art, New York/Scala, Florence (2009 page 6);

The painting 'The Beached Margin' by Edward Wadsworth © Tate, London 2012 (2009 page 7);

Breakfast cereal packaging for ASDA (2007) © ASDA (2009 page 8);

Gramophone designed for Pathé (1908) © The Robert Opie Collection (2009 page 9);

Three photographs of 'Barajas Airport Terminal, Madrid' by Manuel Renau © Aena (2009 page 10);

The photograph 'The Opera House, Paris' by Delagarde and Moatti © Jean-Pierre Delagarde & Jacques Moatti (2009 page 11);

A photograph of a wrist watch designed by Boucheron (1942) © Boucheron (2009 page 12);

A photograph of a Dinosaur coat and hat designed by Zandra Rhodes (1971) © Bishin Jumonji (left) and a photograph of a Dinosaur coat © Zandra Rhodes (right) (2009 page 13);

'The Desperate Man' by Gustave Courbet. Private collection, by courtesy of BNP Paribas Art Advisory (2010 page 2);

The painting 'Gran Turismo' by Megan Davies (2005) © Megan Davies (2010 page 3);

The painting 'Maple and Chocolate' by Ralph Goings (2004) © Ralph Goings (2010 page 4);

The painting 'Frosty Morning, Trow Hill' by Anne Redpath (1935) © Royal Scottish Academy (2010 page 5);

'Street Study outside a School' © Boyle Family. All rights reserved, DACS 2012 (2010 page 6);

'Life' from 'Death Life Hope Fear' 1984 (422 x 250 cm) © Gilbert & George (2010 page 7);

The poster 'Vertigo' designed by Saul Bass. Courtesy of Universal Studios Licensing LLC (2010 page 8);

A picture of Lego © Lego Group Ltd (2010 page 9);

Two photographs of a cookery classroom from Scotland Street School, designed by Charles Rennie Mackintosh (1906) © Martin Smith (2010 page 10);

A photograph of Trellick Tower, London © Edifice www.edificephoto.com (2010 page 11);

A picture of Regenerat, an assembled pendant by Wahei Ikezawa (1994), taken from 'Design Source Book Jewellery' by David Watkins, published by New Holland Publishers (UK) Ltd (2010 page 12);

David Hockney 'My Mother, Bolton Abbey, Yorkshire, Nov. 1982' Photographic Collage, Edition of 20, 47½ x 27½ © David Hockney (2011 page 2);

'The Tennis Party' by John Lavery, taken from Aberdeen Art Gallery & Museums Collections. By courtesy of Felix Rosenstiel's Widow & Son Ltd., London on behalf of the Estate of Sir John Lavery (2011 page 3);

'Table by a Window' by Jean Metzinger © 2011. Image copyright The Metropolitan Museum of Art/Art Resource/Scala, Florence (2011 page 4);

'Cabina NY' by Jose Luis Corella © DACS 2012 (2011 page 6);

'Saint Bride' by John Duncan © Estate of John Duncan. All rights reserved, DACS 2011 (2011 page 7);

Poster for 'The Studio' by Aubrey Beardsley © Victoria and Albert Museum, London (2011 page 8);

Two photos from: http://commons.wikimedia.org/wiki/File:Mini_cross_section.jpg and http://commons.wikimedia.org/wiki/File:Morris_Mini-Minor_1959.jpg. Both licensed under the Creative Commons Attribution-ShareAlike 3.0 Unported Licence (CC BY-SA 3). Details can be viewed at: http://creativecommons.org/licenses/by-sa/3.0/deed.en (2011 page 9);

A photograph of a Topshop store in New York © Dalziel and Pow (2011 page 10);

Three photographs of Maggie's Centre, Dundee. Reproduced with permission of Maggie's Centres (2011 page 11);

Two images of brooches from the Artery series designed by Dorothy Hogg, photographed by John K McGregor © Dorothy Hogg (2011 page 12);

Two images of Platform sandals taken from Victoria and Albert Museum, London © Salvatore Ferragamo (2011 page 13);

'End of the Festival' by David Martin © David Martin (2012 page 2);

'The Third of May 1808' by Francisco Goya © Museo Nacional del Prado (2012 page 3);

'Footdee Winter' by Reinhard Behrens, taken from Aberdeen Art Gallery & Museums Collections © Reinhard Behrens (2012 page 4);

'Leaf Horn' by Andy Goldsworthy © Andy Goldsworthy (2012 page 5);

'Edinburgh (from Salisbury Crags)' by William Crozier, Scottish National Gallery of Modern Art. Copyright National Galleries of Scotland, photography A Reeve (2012 page 6);

A poster © IOC Olympic Museum - Allsport/Getty Images (2012 page 8);

Armchair (1823) designed by Augustus Charles Pugin © Victoria and Albert Museum, London (2012 page 9);

A photograph of Kelvingrove Art Gallery and Museum © CSG CIC Glasgow Museums Collection (2012 page 10);

Millennium Bridge, Gateshead, taken from http://en.wikipedia.org/wiki/File:Gateshead_millennium_bridge_open.jpg (Public Domain) and http://en.wikipedia.org/wiki/File:Gateshead_Millennium_Bridge_close.jpg (Creative Commons Attribution-Share Alike 3.0 Unported) (2012 page 11);

Corsage ornament, 1902 designed by Georges Fouquet © ADAGP, Paris and DACS, London 2012 (2012 page 12);

A photograph © Lewis Whyld/PA Archive/Press Association Images (2012 page 13).

HIGHER | ANSWER SECTION

SQA HIGHER ART & DESIGN
2009–2012

Overview

The Art and Design Studies Examination Paper is set with the following principles in mind:

1. The questions relate to six major aspects of expressive work and six major areas of design reflecting the range of practical work currently engaged in by Art and Design departments.
2. The two parts of each question are set in order to cover critical evaluation (*a*) and historical knowledge and understanding (*b*).
3. Candidates are asked to attempt one full question (parts (*a*) and (*b*)) in both Art Studies and Design Studies to demonstrate their in-depth knowledge of areas selected for their practical work and related study.
4. In Art Studies, part (*a*) of each question will require candidates to analyse and respond to art works in such terms as the visual elements, media handling, communication and meaning, providing personal responses to the work.
5. In Design Studies, part (*a*) of each question will require candidates to comment effectively on aspects such as form, function and communication and the methods and materials used by the designer to achieve them. Personal opinions will also be sought.

   In part (*b*) candidates will require to show an awareness of design issues appropriate to the area of design and demonstrate historical knowledge and understanding of it within the period 1750 to the present.
6. Part (*b*) of each question is intended to be sufficiently open-ended to invite candidates to convey their strengths and interests in their answers while providing enough factual information to convince the marker that their studies have been well researched and their arguments well justified.
7. Specialist knowledge of an identifiable area of the visual arts and of design is therefore a clear requirement in part (*b*) of any question.
8. In Art Studies, in questions where the term 'artist' is used it should be interpreted in its broadest sense, covering painting, printmaking, photography, sculpture, installation, animation, film and video, etc.
9. Similarly in Design Studies questions the term 'designer' should be inclusive of any form of design: graphic design, ceramics, textiles, animation, fashion, illustration, interior design or architecture.

SECTION 1 – ART STUDIES

1. Portraiture

(*a*) In their discussion of the visual impact of the painting, candidates should refer to at least two of the given options. Expect comments about the downward gaze of the figure and the possibly symbolic use of a cross in the background. Also expect comments about the pink and white brushwork which marks out the space where Conroy stands. The symmetry of the composition may be commented upon as well as the strong tonal values in the painting. Tone and colour are used to create a very realistic treatment of the face and hands in particular.

   Any justified opinion of the painting should be rewarded.

(*b*) Knowledge and understanding of portraiture by two artists from different movements or periods should be evident in responses to this question. Particular attention should be given to the artists' choice of subjects and how they have portrayed them. Reference may also be made to styles and working methods.

Full marks are only possible when candidates explain the importance of the artists in the development of portraiture. Four marks should be reserved for that part of their answer.

2. Figure Composition

(*a*) In their discussion of Hanson's approach to figure composition candidates should comment on at least two of the given options.

The interaction of the figures with each other and the viewer may be seen to be successful because of the life size scale and the fact that real clothes and accessories have been used. The composition of the piece may also be seen to assist in that the arrangement suggests a scenario we have all witnessed with tourists. The attention to detail may also add to the success by making the figures appear visually convincing and believable.

(*b*) An in depth study of figure compositions by two artists from different movements or periods should be revealed in candidates' answers. In their discussions of the works, candidates should comment on the working methods used by the artists to commemorate their ideas.

Full marks are only possible when candidates explain the importance of the artists in the development of figure composition. Four marks should be reserved for that part of their answer.

3. Still Life

(*a*) In their analysis of this still life, candidates may comment on the use of mixed media and the loose, expressive style of the work. The random arrangement of objects within the composition may also be seen to be important. The strong monochromatic tones may also be commented upon. The question requires candidates to contrast aspects of the still life they admire with those they think are less successful. Any justified opinion/argument should be rewarded

(*b*) An in depth study of the still life work by two artists from different movements or periods should be evident in candidates' answers. In their discussion of examples of works, candidates should explain why they are typical of each artist's style or associated movement.

Full marks are only possible when candidates explain why the artists are considered important. Four marks should be reserved for that part of their answer.

4. Natural Environment

(*a*) In their discussion of this painting, candidates are required to outline the methods used by McCulloch to create a feeling of grandeur. In doing so they should refer to his use of visual elements. Expect comments on the choice of subject matter which oozes grandeur in its own right! McCulloch's use of strong tonal values creating a dramatic effect and depth in the painting may also be commented upon.

Any justified opinions of the painting should be rewarded.

(*b*) An in depth knowledge of work based on the natural environment should be evident in answers to this question. Candidates should refer to examples by two artists from different movements or periods and should refer to their choice of subject, media handling and style.

Full marks are only possible when candidates explain the importance of the artists in the development of this type of work. Four marks should be reserved for the final part of the question.

5. Built Environment

(a) In discussing the composition of this painting, candidates are required to comment on the artist's media handling and use of visual elements. Expect comments on the strong diagonals in the composition and the use of colour, particularly in the water and on the bridge, to lead the eye around the painting. Candidates may comment on the use of bright colour throughout the work and also the free application of paint. Contrasting tones and the simplification of shape may also be commented upon.

Any justified opinion of the painting should be rewarded.

(b) An in depth study of the work within this theme by two artists from different movements or periods should be evident. In doing so, candidates are required to refer to choice of subject matter, style and working methods.

An explanation of the importance of the artists is required before full marks are awarded. Four marks should be reserved for that part of the question.

6. Fantasy and Imagination

(a) Candidates are required to describe the methods used by Wadsworth to create an unusual scene. Expect comments on the simplified beach composition with sky, sea and sand. In that setting are placed unrelated objects (some with reference to the sea and some not) suspended from posts set at an angle to each other. On top of the posts are shaped cross pieces which may be interpreted as being symbolic. Also in the scene are other objects, some of which are associated with the beach. Strong light casts long shadows on the sand. The scene, unreal though it is, has a very convincing appearance because of the detailed manner in which it is painted.

Any explanation of which aspects of the work candidates find contribute to the success of the work should be rewarded.

(b) Responses to this should be based on an in depth study of two artists' work within this theme. The artists should be from different movements or periods. Brief descriptions of examples by each artist are asked for and candidates are required to discuss the methods used by the artists to create works of fantasy and imagination.

An explanation of the importance of the artists is required before full marks are awarded. Four marks should be reserved for that part of the question.

DESIGN STUDIES

7. Graphic Design

(a) Answers should focus on the way the designer has created visual impact using both colour and tonal contrast. Candidates may also mention that the imagery of 'choco hoops' has been clustered to create one main, eye-catching motif which includes lettering.

In dealing with the issue of communication, candidates should realise that the designer is targeting both parents and children. The designer clearly communicates with the adult audience through clear and simple lettering which gives information to suggest that the product is healthy. However, children are being targeted more obviously through bright colours and attractive imagery which includes sharply defined 'choco hoops' and a 'fun' bird. Justified personal opinions about the success of the design should be rewarded.

(b) Knowledge and understanding of the work of two designers from different periods or styles is expected. Reference should be made to specific examples of their work.

Key aspects such as layout, lettering, imagery and an awareness of how designers communicate their ideas with their target audience should be identified.

There should be a clear indication of the importance of the designers in this area.

Four marks should be reserved for that part of the question.

8. Product Design

(a) Candidates should explain the main design issues to be considered in this example of product design. Function, use of materials and aesthetics should be discussed.

In comparing this gramophone with today's music systems, some candidates may find this design aesthetically pleasing, while others may criticise its old fashioned, ornate qualities. Many candidates will recognise that its styling is Art Nouveau. All should comment on the development of modern technology which has resulted in music systems becoming much more compact, streamlined, versatile and having outstanding sound quality.

(b) Examples of product design by two designers from different periods or styles should be discussed. The designers' consideration of the important design issues listed in the statement should be referred to as they relate to the candidates' chosen examples.

Justification of the designers' importance and their recognition in this area of design will be rewarded with four marks.

9. Interior Design

(a) Answers should mention the open aspect of the space and the use of light, colour and reflective materials which emphasise the sheer size of this terminal. The supporting pillars resemble a giant forest and create a strong element of pattern. The use of natural light from above enhances the shiny, reflective surface textures and creates a sense of light, airy spaciousness.

In discussing the functional aspects of this interior design any justified opinions should be rewarded.

(b) A comparison of two interior designers from different periods or styles is required. Ideas, methods and materials should be discussed along with the intended use of the interiors and how they meet the needs of the client.

Four additional marks would be gained for a clear indication of the designers' importance and influence in interior design.

10. Architecture/Environmental Design

(a) Responses should focus on the extremely ornate and elaborate appearance of The Opera House, Paris and some candidates may realise that this building is an extravagant, opulent symbol of wealth and power. Reference should be made to the symmetry of decoration created by the architect's use of pillars and arches. The classical influence may be recognised. It should be noted that this building would have required highly skilled artists to create the elaborate relief decoration and sculptures.

In discussing the function of this opera house, candidates should refer to issues such as acoustics and the size of the auditorium. Mention might be made of the large, paved area at the entrance which would have been suitable, even in The Opera's early days of horses and carriages, for dropping off and picking up opera goers.

(b) A comparison of the work of two architects/environmental designers from different periods or styles is required. Candidates should discuss materials, the aesthetic qualities and the function of their chosen examples. There should be a clear indication of the standing and importance of the designers in this area which would gain four marks.

11. Jewellery Design

(a) Candidates should refer to the designer's use of precious metal and stones which would make this wristwatch a very expensive one-off piece. In discussing the designer's handling of form, candidates may refer to the unusual structure of the piece and may recognise the Art Deco styling or even the Egyptian influence.

Any consideration of function eg the "easy to wear" flexible bracelet will be relevant.

(b) References to the work of two jewellery designers from different periods or styles are required. Explanation of their sources of inspiration and how they have developed their ideas for jewellery should be given.

An understanding of the materials and working methods used by the designers is expected.

Reasons for their importance as jewellery designers should be awarded with four marks.

12. Textile/Fashion Design

(a) Answers should refer to the designer's use of wool, lined with satin, which would be warm, comfortable and luxurious to wear. The off-white colour is impractical but adds to the luxurious appearance of the outfit.

Reference may be made to the hat which appears to be decorative rather than functional. The unusual styling of the coat is an important element and candidates would be expected to comment on the scalloped structure and the appliqué decoration.

Most answers should mention that natural form is the most obvious source of inspiration. Some may recognise the influence of Matisse.

Any justified opinion of this outfit should be rewarded.

(b) A good knowledge of the work of two textile or fashion designers from different periods or styles is required. Candidates should discuss the ways in which their chosen designers have shown innovation. Referring to examples of their work, they should explain their working methods, choice of materials and style.

Four marks will be awarded for justification of the designers' influence in this area of design.

HIGHER ART AND DESIGN 2010

Overview

The Art and Design Studies Examination Paper is set with the following principles in mind:

1. The questions relate to six major aspects of expressive work and six major areas of design reflecting the range of practical work currently engaged in by Art and Design departments.

2. The two parts of each question are set in order to cover critical evaluation (a) and historical knowledge and understanding (b).

3. Candidates are asked to attempt one full question (parts (a) and (b)) in both Art Studies and Design Studies to demonstrate their in-depth knowledge of areas selected for their practical work and related study.

4. In Art Studies, part (a) of each question will require candidates to analyse and respond to art works in such terms as the visual elements, media handling, communication and meaning, providing personal responses to the work.

5. In Design Studies, part (a) of each question will require candidates to comment effectively on aspects such as form, function and communication and the methods and materials used by the designer to achieve them. Personal opinions will also be sought.

In part (b) candidates will require to show an awareness of design issues appropriate to the area of design and demonstrate historical knowledge and understanding of it within the period 1750 to the present.

6. Part (b) of each question is intended to be sufficiently open-ended to invite candidates to convey their strengths and interests in their answers while providing enough factual information to convince the marker that their studies have been well researched and their arguments well justified.

7. Specialist knowledge of an identifiable area of the visual arts and of design is therefore a clear requirement in part (b) of any question.

8. In Art Studies, in questions where the term 'artist' is used it should be interpreted in its broadest sense, covering painting, printmaking, photography, sculpture, installation, animation, film and video, etc.

9. Similarly in Design Studies questions the term 'designer' should be inclusive of any form of design: graphic design, ceramics, textiles, animation, fashion, illustration, interior design or architecture.

SECTION 1 – ART STUDIES

1. Portraiture

(a) Justified personal responses about what the artist is communicating to us should be rewarded. A detailed analysis of the painting should include a reference to Courbet's use of the visual elements within the work, eg the dramatic effect of the source of light on the left and the rich glow, which it creates.

Comments by the candidates on any two or more of the following should be rewarded:

Pose
Tone
Composition
Mood
Media Handling

Justified personal opinion should also be well rewarded.

(b) Answers should refer to portraits by two artists from different periods or movements. Candidates should show an understanding of their contrasting styles. Marks should be awarded for comments on the artists' use of composition and the visual elements. Full marks are only possible when an explanation of the artists in the development of portraiture is stated.

2. Figure Composition

(a) Candidates should be rewarded for comments on the unusual composition of the painting, eg the strong horizontal of the sofa, which is broken by the angular figures and the low viewpoint, contributes to the drama of this artwork.

Comments by the candidates on any two or more of the following should also be rewarded:

Setting
Mood
Media Handling
Colour
Tone

Any justified opinion on the inter-relationship between the figures should gain marks.

(b) Answers should refer to figure composition by two artists from different periods or movements. Candidates should show an understanding of their contrasting styles and working methods. Responses, which justify the importance of the artists' contribution to the development of figure composition, should be rewarded.

3. Still Life

(a) The question requires the candidate to make an analysis of the composition, eg the carefully balanced forms and the use of perspective. Comment should be made about the artist's handling of media, colour and tone with reference to this work being a traditional approach to a modern subject matter. Candidates should also note the artist's use of a full tonal range and the use of warm and cool colours. Justified personal opinion should be rewarded.

(b) Answers should refer to still life work by two artists from different periods or movements. Candidates should show an understanding of their contrasting styles. Marks should be awarded for comments on the artists' use of composition and media handling. Full marks are only possible when an explanation of the artists' contribution to the development of still life is explained.

4. Natural Environment

(a) Justified opinions on how successful the artist has been, in creating a sense of atmosphere, should be rewarded. Candidates should mention the composition, use of colour and media handling, eg the use of perspective to lead the viewer's eye into the composition and the careful balance of the group of trees on the left, with the houses and hills on the right.

A personal response to the artwork should be well rewarded.

(b) Answers should refer to two artists from different periods or movements who have produced work inspired by the natural environment. Candidates should show an understanding of their contrasting styles. Marks should be awarded for comments on the artists' working methods. Full marks are only possible when an explanation of the artists' contribution to the development of this genre is stated.

5. Built Environment

(a) Reference to the commonplace nature of the subject should feature in a strong response. A detailed analysis of this artwork should include a reference to the Boyle

Family's use of materials, scale, colour and texture. Reference should also be made to the realistic quality of this piece. Discussion of the technical difficulties of casting this work should be rewarded.

Justified personal opinions of this method of working should also be well rewarded.

(b) Answers should refer to the study of works by two artists, from different periods or movements, who are inspired by the built environment. Candidates should show an understanding of their working methods and their ability to create a sense of atmosphere. Full marks are only possible, when a candidate explains the importance of these artists in the development of artwork inspired by the built environment.

6. Fantasy and Imagination

(a) Justified personal responses about the artists' use of composition and discussion of the content of this artwork should be rewarded, eg the virtually symmetrical nature of the composition and the stained glass like effect of the piece. Comment is also expected on the artists' use of colour and pattern, eg the use of strong complimentary colours and repeated shapes. Justified personal interpretation of the piece should be well rewarded.

(b) Responses should be based upon works by two artists from different periods or movements working within this theme. Comments on the use of imagery to communicate ideas should be rewarded. Full marks are only possible when an explanation of the artists' contribution to the development of fantasy and imagination is given.

SECTION 2 – DESIGN STUDIES

7. Graphic Design

(a) In discussing the use of <u>colour</u> in creating visual impact, candidates should refer to the designer's use of red in the background which, combined with the use of black and white in the foreground, is extremely eye catching. The use of a limited palette may be commented on.

In commenting on the poster's <u>imagery</u>, candidates should be aware of the designer's use of flattened, stylized motifs. Clustering imagery in one dramatic, swirling spiral draws the viewer into the design and is visually compelling. Answers should note that <u>lettering</u> has been kept to a minimum.
By using a simple lettering style in black, placed against the red background, the designer enhances the visual impact of the poster.

In discussing the <u>ideas communicated</u> through this poster, candidates will respond in many ways, eg
- The use of red might suggest fear or danger.
- The main spiral motif might convey the idea of falling associated with vertigo.
- The spiral motif resembles the barrel of a gun. This communicates a sense of danger.
- The layout of the flattened figures suggests the idea of a chase.
- The solid black motif of the male figure might suggest the body in a murder scene.
- The 'hand written' font, combined with flattened imagery, creates a cartoon-like quality which could be seen to lighten the mood.
Any well justified comments should be rewarded.

(b) Examples of graphic design by two designers from different periods or working in different styles should be referred to in discussing the main priorities for graphic designers.

Visual impact, communication, lettering, lay-out and target market are the main issues which candidates should be aware of. Answers should give a clear indication of why the candidate believes the designers to be influential.

8. Product Design

(a) Candidates should explain what they think are the main design issues which were considered by the designers eg

- Designing an educational construction toy which, by encouraging creativity in children of different ages, would appeal to the target market of parents.
- Designing a strong, hard-wearing, safe, hygienic toy which could withstand rough treatment.
- Ensuring the interlocking system was strong enough to assemble but not too strong for children to disassemble.
- Producing a bright, attractive building system to appeal to children of most ages.

In discussing why Lego is still successful, candidates might deduce that, as a problem-solving toy, it continues to appeal to parents or that children continue to enjoy the opportunities to be creative which it provides. They might suggest that colours have changed in recent years to keep up with changing trends or that a chunkier, simpler version (Duplo) appeared in the 1980's to appeal to parents of younger children. Any well justified reasons should be rewarded.

(b) Examples of work by two product designers from different periods or styles should be compared, showing the candidate's grasp of the historical background, design issues and how the designers have affected the daily lives of the client group. Answers should give a clear indication of how important the candidate considers the designers to be in the development of product design.

9. Interior Design

(a) Candidates are expected to comment on design issues in interior design such as the intended use for the space and meeting the needs of the clients. Safety and cost might be considered along with the designer's use of materials available at the time. Aesthetic issues such as space and style should also be discussed.

In discussing how this cookery room differs from it's present day equivalent, candidates should be rewarded for any justified opinions on changing styles, materials and developments in technology which have taken place.

(b) A good knowledge of the work of two interior designers working in different styles or periods is required. Candidates should show an awareness of their sources of inspiration and materials. Their knowledge and understanding of this area of design should enable them to outline how changing fashions might have influenced the designers too. There should be a clear indication of the importance of the designers in this area.

10. Environmental/Architectural Design

(a) In discussing the statement, candidates are required to consider the intended function of this building and whether the architect has been successful in meeting the needs of his clients. A good answer will discuss issues such as living conditions and will question the concept of high-rise dwelling flats eg is it acceptable for people to live in box-like apartments contained in concrete tower blocks in such close proximity to hundreds of people living in identical flats? Reference to further practical issues such as dependency on often malfunctioning elevators would gain marks along with any other justified opinion on the architect's use of materials. Candidates should also discuss the aesthetics and style of the building. All well argued comments will be rewarded.

(b) Responses should show a clear understanding of the work of two architects or environmental designers from different periods or who work in different styles.
Candidates should make clear reference to influences, working methods, aesthetics and innovation in their discussion of the characteristics of their work. Answers should justify the importance of the two designers.

11. Jewellery Design

(a) In discussing the designer's sources of inspiration and use of materials in creating this pendant, answers should refer to the strong influence of machinery and the resulting mechanical or industrial aesthetics of the neck piece. Candidates should comment on the designer's working methods recognising that the pendant has been assembled using found objects. In discussing the practicality of the pendant candidates should note the size of the piece and deduce that this, combined with the weight of the materials used, would strongly affect the wearability of the pendant.

(b) Examples of jewellery design by two designers from different periods or styles should be discussed.
An understanding of their influences, working methods and styles is required in discussing examples of their jewellery design. Justification of the designers' importance and recognition in this area of design will be awarded.

12. Textile/Fashion Design

(a) There is much to discuss in this typical designer outfit of the period. The form and function should be addressed and all relevant comment regarding the variety of textural ideas, the different approaches used in constructing the elements of the outfit and the rhythmical movements sculpted around the body will be rewarded.
A good answer will notice that the designer concentrates on the coexistence of the fabric and the body, which is linked by movement, and that he is involved with identifying the space between the body and the outfit. This would gain high marks.

(b) Responses to this question might include a demonstrated knowledge of fashion, costume design, fabrics (printed/constructed), etc and answers would be expected to discuss, in some detail, specific examples of work by the selected designers. Full marks can only be achieved when responses attempt to justify the importance of the designers in the context of the development of textile design.

HIGHER ART AND DESIGN 2011

Overview

The Art and Design Studies Examination Paper is set with the following principles in mind:

1. The questions relate to six major aspects of expressive work and six major areas of design reflecting the range of practical work currently engaged in by Art and Design departments.
2. The two parts of each question are set in order to cover critical evaluation (a) and historical knowledge and understanding (b).
3. Candidates are asked to attempt one full question (parts (a) and (b)) in both Art Studies and Design Studies to demonstrate their in-depth knowledge of areas selected for their practical work and related study.
4. In Art Studies, part (a) of each question will require candidates to analyse and respond to art works in such terms as the visual elements, media handling, communication and meaning, providing personal responses to the work.
5. In Design Studies, part (a) of each question will require candidates to comment effectively on aspects such as form, function and communication and the methods and materials used by the designer to achieve them. Personal opinions will also be sought.
   In part (b) candidates will require to show an awareness of design issues appropriate to the area of design and demonstrate historical knowledge and understanding of it within the period 1750 to the present.
6. Part (b) of each question is intended to be sufficiently open-ended to invite candidates to convey their strengths and interests in their answers while providing enough factual information to convince the marker that their studies have been well researched and their arguments well justified.
7. Specialist knowledge of an identifiable area of the visual arts and of design is therefore a clear requirement in part (b) of any question.
8. In Art Studies, in questions where the term 'artist' is used it should be interpreted in its broadest sense, covering painting, printmaking, photography, sculpture, installation, animation, film and video, etc.
9. Similarly in Design Studies questions the term 'designer' should be inclusive of any form of design: graphic design, ceramics, textiles, animation, fashion, illustration, interior design or architecture.

SECTION 1 – ART STUDIES

1. Portraiture

(a) A detailed analysis of the work should include reference to Hockney's statement and his use of the visual elements, eg the choice of location in relation to the character of the sitter and the unique collage like approach to this portrait. Some candidates may link the use of multiple viewpoints with the Cubist style. Justified personal responses to the artist's approach to portraiture will be rewarded.

(b) Answers should refer to portraits by **two** artists from different periods or movements. Candidates should show an understanding of their chosen artists' working methods and styles. Marks will be awarded for comments on the artists' exploration of character in their portraits. Full marks are only possible when an explanation of the artists' significance in the development of portraiture is stated.

2. Figure Composition

(a) Candidates will be rewarded for comments on the unusual dimensions and composition of the painting, with reference to the relationship between the figures.

Comments by candidates on the artist's working methods eg form, tone and colour in creating a sense of movement and atmosphere will be well rewarded. Well-justified personal opinions about the overall success of this artwork will also gain marks.

(b) Answers should refer to figure compositions by **two** artists from different periods or movements. Candidates should show an understanding of their contrasting styles and make reference to their choice of subject matter and use of the visual elements. Full marks are only possible when responses, which justify the importance of the artists' contribution to the development of figure composition, are stated.

3. Still Life

(a) The question requires the candidate to make an analysis of this non-traditional approach to still life eg Cubist style – use of multi-point perspective and geometric forms. Candidates should comment on two or more of the following:

composition
colour
form
tone

Personal views regarding this artwork, in relation to more traditional approaches to still life, should be well justified and rewarded accordingly.

(b) Answers should refer to still life work by **two** artists from different periods or movements. Candidates should show an understanding of their choice of subject matter. Marks will be awarded for comments on the artists' use of composition and media handling. Full marks are only possible when an explanation of the artists' importance in the development of still life is explained.

4. Natural Environment

(a) Justified opinions about the visual impact of the artwork will be rewarded. Candidates should mention the composition, use of perspective, colour, sense of atmosphere and media handling eg the unusual viewpoint. Some may also observe that the hunter is not the focal point despite the title of the piece.

Personal responses in regard to the success of this artwork will also be well rewarded.

(b) Answers should refer to **two** artists from different periods or movements, who have produced work inspired by the natural environment. Candidates should show an understanding of the innovative nature of their styles. Strong responses should make reference to the quote. Marks will be awarded for comments on the artists' use of the visual elements. Full marks are only possible when an explanation of the artists' significance in the development of this genre is explained.

5. Built Environment

(a) Reference to the city centre nature of the subject should feature in a strong response. A detailed analysis of this artwork should include reference to the artist's use of composition and perspective. Candidates should discuss the artist's working methods in relation to creating a sense of atmosphere. It would be hoped that by reading the legend, they will realise that this is not a photograph but a painting. Justified personal opinions in relation to the success of this artwork will also be well rewarded.

(b) Answers should refer to the study of works by **two** artists from different periods or movements, who have been inspired by the built environment. Candidates should show an understanding of their use of the visual elements and their ability to create a sense of mood in their work. Full marks are only possible, when a candidate explains each artist's contribution to the development of artwork inspired by the built environment.

6. Fantasy and Imagination

(a) Discussion of the artist's working methods in the creation of this artwork will be rewarded. Reference should be made to the artist's use of composition, pattern, colour, atmosphere and media handling eg the rich use of colour, adding to the mystical subject matter of the piece and the use of strong diagonal lines in the composition. Justified personal opinions about the artist's approach to the subject matter will be well rewarded.

(b) Responses should be based upon works by **two** artists from different periods or movements working within this area. Comments on the artists' choice of theme and working methods will be rewarded. Full marks are only possible when an explanation of both artists' impact in the development of fantasy and imagination is made.

SECTION 2 – DESIGN STUDIES

7. Graphic Design

(a) Imagery – candidates may recognise that the imagery is typical of the Art Nouveau style. Trees and flowers have been stylised to appear elegant and decorative. They are intricate and complex but have been clustered to create a visually compelling design. The monochromatic colour scheme creates tonal contrast which is eye-catching.

Lettering – candidates should comment on the variety of fonts and sizes used which makes the lettering interesting and an integral element of the overall design. Attention is brought to the title and price of the magazine as a bolder font has been used to convey the most important information.

Layout – Beardsley has arranged imagery and lettering within compartments and banners. This creates a sense of order and prevents the design from appearing too busy and complicated.

The design has been created by hand whereas most modern graphic designs are created using technology such as photography and computer-generated imagery and lettering. Candidates may comment that the formal layout is dated. The style of lettering is also quite different. The lack of colour should also be mentioned.

(b) Candidates should demonstrate knowledge and understanding of the work of **two** designers from different periods or styles by referring to specific examples of their work. An awareness of how they have communicated their ideas with their target market should be shown. Key aspects such as lettering and imagery should be discussed. An understanding of the importance of the designers in the development of graphics should be demonstrated in order to gain 4 marks approx.

8. Product Design

(a) Function – cheap to buy – easy to maintain – economical to run – easy to park – some candidates may feel it is too small – other may realise (from the cross-section) that it is surprisingly spacious, seating 4 adults – small boot however – small wheels and low suspension enables it to hold the road tightly.

Style – simple, geometric and compact – typical of late fifties and early sixties style. Cute appearance appealing to wide target market including young people and especially girls – Available in different colours to create a different 'look'.

In discussing the reasons for the endurance and success of the Mini, candidates should refer to issues such as target market, aesthetics, cost and function. Any responses which give good reasons for the Mini's lasting popularity will be rewarded.

(b) Examples of product designs by **two** designers from different periods or styles should be discussed, with particular reference to the candidate's ideas on successful product design from the customer's point of view. Any thoughtful response to the second part of the question will be awarded up to 4 marks.

9. Interior Design

(a) Key issues which may be identified by candidates are space, cost, materials, display potential, target market.

Structure – candidates should comment on the openness of the structure which creates a light, airy, contemporary space while some may recognise that the pillars create a classical, up-market image. The signs indicate that there are other floors situated within the overall structure. The display areas are created using block-like structures which appear to be versatile and can probably be constructed and rearranged easily to create a new look.

Materials – candidates should comment on the designer's use of glass, steel, plastic and lots of light-reflective materials which add to the feeling of a bright contemporary interior space.

Lighting – varied, multi-directional lighting for example spotlights to highlight certain areas, recessed lighting and natural light from windows all create a contemporary mood.

Any justified opinion of this interior design will be rewarded.

(b) Knowledge and understanding of the work of **two** designers from different periods or styles is expected. Reference should be made to specific examples of their work to clearly indicate their importance in this area. Candidates should explain how the designers' styles have evolved through the ways in which they have used their sources of inspiration and creativity.

10. Environmental/Architectural Design

(a) Form combined with function – the spiky jagged forms of the overhanging rooftops contrast in an interesting way with the curving facades of the building and would be functionally effective in dealing with rain and snow. They also shelter the terrace which allows visitors and patients to enjoy an outside space with beautiful views in all weathers. The rear façade is almost cottage-like creating a homely, welcoming environment. The curved tower would create an aesthetically pleasing interior space with large windows which give a great outlook for people using the centre, as the views across the river would be spectacular.

In comparing this centre aesthetically to other medical centres, surgeries or hospitals, candidates would be expected to comment on the dramatic site with exceptional views and rural surroundings which is unusual in buildings of this type. They might also consider this rich and varied design by Gehry to be much more exciting and original than the conventional straight-edged box-like designs of most modern hospitals or health centres and very different to the ornate imposing style of outdated Victorian hospital buildings which they may be familiar with. Any justified comparison will be rewarded.

(b) Examples of the work of **two** designers in this area should be discussed to show the candidate's understanding of their vision and working methods and how they have contributed to the development of environmental or architectural design. There should be a clear indication of the standing or importance of the designers in order to gain 4 marks.

11. Jewellery Design

(a) Sources of inspiration – candidates should be aware of the designer's use of natural form as a source of inspiration – in particular the human body and the idea of blood flowing through arteries. Candidates may comment on similarities of natural inspiration to Art Nouveau design or recognise the influence of Art Deco in the basic geometric structure of the brooches.

Handling of form – the tubular forms are linear and fluid in appearance however the basic structure is a geometric ring which is echoed in other areas and details of the designs.

Choice of materials – silver is crisp and clean and has a contemporary look. The use of coral reflects the 'artery' theme suggesting blood.

Any justified opinion on what the candidate considers to be the most striking features of the designs will be rewarded.

(b) Reference to the work of **two** jewellery designers from different periods or styles is required. Candidates should discuss the ways in which their chosen designers have shown originality and dealt with the issues of function and style. 4 marks will be awarded for justification of the designers' influence in this area of design.

12. Textile/Fashion Design

(a) Key design issues – in identifying these, candidates should focus on style and function. They may also mention target market, cost and use of materials.
Candidates should, in discussing the designer's ideas, make reference to how successfully he has dealt with the key issues.

Style – candidates will probably recognise the Art Deco style in the geometric structure of the sandals and the vividly coloured rainbow effect of the layered platforms and heavy use of gold. Some may comment on how contemporary the sandals look and realise that this style has continued to influence today's shoe designers and that because of this the design is highly effective.

Function – questions should arise about the practicality of these sandals. They would have limited wearability because of their height. However the use of cork would make them light to wear. The use of straps and buckles would make them more practical as the wearer's feet would be held firmly in place.

Candidates should realise that part of their function would be to lend height to the wearer and that the designer did not intend them to be 'everyday' sandals. They have been designed to create impact for a special occasion.

Other issues – these shoes would have been expensive – a one-off design for a wealthy target market.

(b) Candidates should show knowledge and understanding of the work and development of **two** fashion/textile designers from different periods or styles. Answers should explain how the designers have adapted to quickly changing trends and how they have created innovative fashion or textile designs. Candidates should explain why the designers are important in order to attain 4 marks.

HIGHER ART AND DESIGN 2012

Overview

The Art and Design Studies Examination Paper is set with the following principles in mind:

1. The questions relate to six major aspects of expressive work and six major areas of design reflecting the range of practical work currently engaged in by Art and Design departments.

2. The two parts of each question are set in order to cover critical evaluation (a) and historical knowledge and understanding (b).

3. Candidates are asked to attempt one full question (parts (a) and (b)) in both Art Studies and Design Studies to demonstrate their in-depth knowledge of areas selected for their practical work and related study.

4. In Art Studies, part (a) of each question will require candidates to analyse and respond to art works in such terms as the visual elements, media handling, communication and meaning, providing personal responses to the work.

5. In Design Studies, part (a) of each question will require candidates to comment effectively on aspects such as form, function and communication and the methods and materials used by the designer to achieve them. Personal opinions will also be sought.

   In part (b) candidates will require to show an awareness of design issues appropriate to the area of design and demonstrate historical knowledge and understanding of it within the period 1750 to the present.

6. Part (b) of each question is intended to be sufficiently open-ended to invite candidates to convey their strengths and interests in their answers while providing enough factual information to convince the marker that their studies have been well researched and their arguments well justified.

7. Specialist knowledge of an identifiable area of the visual arts and of design is therefore a clear requirement in part (b) of any question.

8. In Art Studies, in questions where the term 'artist' is used it should be interpreted in its broadest sense, covering painting, printmaking, photography, sculpture, installation, animation, film and video, etc.

9. Similarly in Design Studies questions the term 'designer' should be inclusive of any form of design: graphic design, ceramics, textiles, animation, fashion, illustration, interior design or architecture.

SECTION 1 – ART STUDIES

1. Portraiture

(a) This question should allow the candidate to discuss the composition of this piece. They should further comment on the artist's use of colour and pattern in David Martin's painting to gain full marks. A good answer should include an attempt to make some interpretation surrounding the title of the work.

The candidate may use first hand knowledge of attending a festival and will be rewarded fully for this. Additional comments which explore the sitter's relationship with the viewer will be rewarded fully.

Any other justified comment will be rewarded.

(b) Responses to this question should reflect an in-depth study of **two** artists' work within portraiture. The artists should be from different movements or periods. Candidates must refer to specific artworks when discussing inspiration, working methods and the appearance and character of the sitters. Four marks are allocated to the final part of the

question and candidates should refer to examples. Full marks cannot be awarded unless the final part of the question has been answered.

2. Figure Composition

(a) This part of the question should provoke a range of valid personal responses about the situation portrayed in this work. To gain full marks the candidate's response should attempt to discuss the subject with direct reference to the composition.

The action takes place in the bottom half of the painting away from the view of the town.

The area of colour and lighting should again be discussed with justification.

Candidates may comment on the repeated poses of the faceless executioners.

This is in contrast to the poses of the insurgents who vary from pleading, hiding, praying to defiance. The figure with his arms raised is brighter and disproportionately taller than the other figures in the painting; this with the brightness of his clothes makes him more apparent. In the candidate's response the personal opinion of their thoughts and feelings on this strongly graphic subject will be noted and fully rewarded.

Any other justified comment will be rewarded.

(b) Candidate answers should reflect as in-depth a study of figure composition from **two** artists from different movements or periods. In their discussion of specific works, candidates should mention inspiration as well as approaches and working methods that led to successful depictions of human interactions. Four marks are allocated to the final part of the question and candidates should refer to examples. Full marks cannot be awarded unless the final part of the question has been answered fully.

3. Still Life

(a) The question requires candidates to make an analysis of this unusual approach to still life. Comments should be made on the careful positioning of 'found' objects, ones probably washed up on the shore, which create a balanced composition. Candidates may speculate that the artist has gathered these items whilst beach-combing and decided to draw them.

Most candidates will probably comment on the photographic quality of this piece and the unusual layout. Some may make a reference to Will MacLean's boxed pieces or some of Elizabeth Blackadder's still lifes, but this would not be essential to gain full marks. Comments should be made on the muted palette, dictated by the 'washed out' objects and the careful alternating of pale rust/orange with blue/grey objects. Some might observe that the drawing of the village and harbour is the least realistic image there. Candidates must make a reference to all parts of the question to gain full marks. Personal views regarding this artwork should be well justified and will be rewarded accordingly.

(b) Responses to this question should show an in depth study of **two** artists working in the area of still life. Candidates should make reference to the quote, either supporting or refuting the statement. Candidates should discuss specific artworks and describe in detail the artists' working methods. Four marks are allocated to the final part of the question and candidates should refer to examples. Full marks cannot be awarded unless the final part of the question has been answered fully.

4. Natural Environment

(a) This part of the question should provoke a range of valid responses to this piece of environmental sculpture. Candidates may make observations on the immediacy of this piece, the use of found materials and may pick up that it is held together with just thorns and nothing else. They may also comment on the relationship of the piece created to the space it occupies and the surrounding area. The transience of such a piece may also be commented on; how long will it last, who might see it, what is its inspiration? A reasoned opinion on how this piece challenges the traditional norm in the genre will be well rewarded.

(b) Candidates should show an in-depth knowledge of the working methods of **two** artists working in the area of the natural environment from different styles or time periods. Candidates should make detailed reference to different approaches and sources of inspiration. Full marks are only possible when the candidate has explained why these artists are influential with reference to specific examples. Four marks are awarded for the final part of the question.

5. Built Environment

(a) Reference to the characterful and dramatic nature of the city scene should feature in a strong response. A detailed analysis of this artwork should refer to the artist's use of the visual elements e.g. the strong use of contrasting tone and the angular forms of the dark city buildings in contrast to the smoother lighter forms of the countryside. In a strong answer, candidates should also discuss the artist's handling of materials/use of brush strokes. Justified personal opinions of this work will also be well rewarded. Candidates may write good personal opinions of perceived weaknesses.

(b) Candidates should demonstrate an in depth knowledge of the work of **two** artists from different styles or time periods working in this area. Candidates should discuss in detail sources of inspiration and working methods with reference to specific examples. These examples should be referred to each artist's style or movement. Four marks are reserved for the final part of the question. Candidates should describe in detail, with reference to examples, the importance and influence of each artist. Full marks are only possible if the candidate has answered fully the final part.

6. Fantasy and Imagination

(a) Any justified opinion of the success of the sculpture should be rewarded but a very good answer would take into account the sitting of the sculpture and the impact of its large scale. Reference to the symbolism involved in placing the figure of an angel above a town would also be expected in very good answers.

(b) Responses to this should be based on an in-depth study of two artists' work within this theme and from different movements or periods.
Candidates should refer to examples of work and discuss the methods used by the artists to communicate their ideas. Full marks can only be gained when candidates explain the extent of the artists' influence in the development of this type of work.

SECTION 2 – DESIGN STUDIES

7. Graphic Design

(a) The main ideas are strength, power, speed and glory. In discussing the success of the design candidates should consider **at least two** of the following:

Imagery
(1) The image of the strong Grecian athlete rising above the building conveys a sense of power and strength.
(2) The use of the Olympic symbol is instantly recognizable.
(3) The strong black shape of the building and horses has visual impact and conveys strength and movement.

Layout
(1) Changing the scale of the athlete to appear enormous is very eye-catching.
(2) Candidates might notice that the light lettering has visual impact against the dark background.
(3) The Olympic symbol is large and easy to see.

Text
(1) Classical style of lettering echoes the Grecian tradition of the games.
(2) Information is kept to a minimum.
(3) It is clear and easy to read.

Colour
(1) The gold suggests the Olympic flame and the glory of the gold medal.

Visual Impact
(1) The dramatic contrast between the black area and the gold area is very eye-catching. Any other justified personal opinions will be well rewarded.

(b) Candidates should demonstrate in-depth knowledge of the work of **two** graphic designers working in different styles or time periods. Candidates should discuss the design issues of specific graphic designs and include detailed analysis of the use of text and layout. They should also discuss the designers' success in communicating. The candidates should use specific examples to explain their chosen designers' importance and influence; four marks are allocated to this final part of the question. Full marks cannot be awarded unless the final part of the question is answered fully.

8. Product Design

(a) Function – the chair is functionally sound as the padded upholstery would provide comfort. The gently sloping backrest would provide support for the back and the arms have an ergonomic quality.

Style – the style is fussier and more elaborate than today's furniture design. Candidates might recognise historical influences such as Gothic stained glass windows or Egyptian thrones. The overall appearance is rich and luxurious.

Target market – this chair is aimed at a wealthy clientele as it is a one-off design which features the highest standard of craftsmanship and materials.
Any other justified personal opinions will be well rewarded

(b) Candidates should demonstrate an in-depth understanding of the work of **two** product designers working in different styles or time periods. Using examples of their work, candidates should show knowledge of design issues such as technology, innovation, use of materials, form, function and market place. Candidates should refer to specific examples in the final section of the question in order to answer it fully. Four marks are allocated to the final section.

9. Interior Design

(a) Key issues which may be identified by candidates:

Space – large open space with soaring heights enable the museum to display very large exhibits simultaneously, for example an aeroplane and a giraffe. The space is used to create easy access for visitors with clear views of the exhibits.

Materials – the tiled pattern floor is attractive, hard-wearing and easily cleaned. The sandstone has allowed the stonemasons to create a complex interior design. Candidates may mention the wooden display systems installed during the recent refurbishment.

Structure – the designers have used an elaborate system of columns and arches. Candidates may recognise the classical influences of the design. The structure has been used to create a series of walkways and corridors.

Lighting - artificial lighting is evident and seems to be effective in illuminating exhibits.

Any justified opinions about how effective the design is as an exhibition space will be rewarded.

(b) Candidates should demonstrate an in-depth knowledge of the work of **two** interior designers working in different styles or time periods. They should use specific examples to show understanding of the design issues involved such as lighting, surface, space, technology, innovation and fitness for purpose. The candidates should use specific examples to explain their chosen designers' importance and influence; four marks are allocated to this final part of the question. Full marks cannot be awarded unless the final part of the question is answered fully.

10. Environmental/Architectural Design

(a) Candidates should evaluate the success of the design solution in relation to key design issues.

Issues identified may include function – to provide a link between the two sides of the river for pedestrians while allowing boats to pass underneath and how the form of the bridge makes this possible. It is clear that a great deal of structural engineering is involved in the mechanism which allows the bridge to be raised and lowered. Aesthetics (style/sources of inspiration/influences/how the bridge integrates with its surroundings) may be discussed.

Some disadvantages may be observed, such as how the curvilinear form requires pedestrians to walk further than they would have to if the bridge was straight. Pedestrians may also have to wait at time, while boats pass underneath. Well justified points relating to the question will be rewarded.

(b) Candidates should demonstrate in-depth knowledge of the work of **two** designers working in different styles or time periods. Candidates should discuss the design issued of specific designs and include detailed analysis of use of materials and form. They should discuss the innovative aspects of their chosen designers' work. The candidates should use specific examples to explain their chosen designers' importance and influence; four marks are allocated to this final part of the question. Full marks cannot be awarded unless the final part of the question is answered fully.

11. Jewellery Design

(a) Influences- mythology, natural form, Japanese, Celtic Craftsmanship – intricate detail, sophisticated enamelling and setting techniques requiring a high level of skill.

Use of materials – precious materials like gold and emeralds, plus the time required to produce such an intricate piece would make this very expensive.

Style – typically Art Nouveau with elongated twisting forms based on nature. This is a very elegant piece.

This brooch might be appealing to today's fashion market as there has been a recent revival of intricate delicate jewellery.

Candidates might also make references to the size and functional aspects of wearing this brooch. Any other justified personal opinions will be well rewarded.

(b) Candidates should discuss specific examples of work by **two** designers working in different time periods or styles. The work chosen should showcase the designers' skill and use of materials. Candidates should provide detailed commentary of working methods and a clear understanding of the designers' clientele. The candidate should use specific examples to explain their chosen designers' importance and influence; four marks are allocated to this final part of the question. Full marks cannot be awarded unless the final part of the question is answered fully.

12. Textile/Fashion Design

(a) Design issues – fitness for purpose eg wearability and practicality of materials, style and colour, should have visual appeal for staff and customers.

Improvements – more sophisticated style and colour suggesting efficiency or executive styling.

Candidates might note that employees self esteem would rise as a result of wearing this uniform. The uniform has a more positive image than the old uniform which suggests a more unskilled role. Candidates might however consider the clerical colours to be more drab and less fun than the older uniform. They might see the neckerchief as more of an obstruction for the wearer.

Well reasoned positive and negative comments will be rewarded.

(b) Candidates should comment fully on the work of **two** different fashion/textile designers working in different styles or time periods. They should demonstrate an in-depth knowledge of the relevant design issues such as use of materials, fitness for purpose, cost and method of manufacture and how these aspects contributed to the success of the designs. The candidates should discuss the designers' use of innovation through their working methods and approaches. the candidates should use specific examples to explain their chosen designers' importance and influence; four marks are allocated to this final part of the question. Full marks cannot be awarded unless the final part of the question is answered fully.

Hey! I've done it

© 2012 SQA/Bright Red Publishing Ltd, All Rights Reserved
Published by Bright Red Publishing Ltd, 6 Stafford Street, Edinburgh, EH3 7AU
Tel: 0131 220 5804, Fax: 0131 220 6710, enquiries: sales@brightredpublishing.co.uk,
www.brightredpublishing.co.uk

Official SQA answers to 978-1-84948-281-3
2009-2012